CONTENTS

STRAIGHT A LAW STUDENT
series

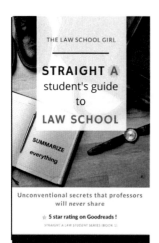

PART I

Study very efficiently like a straight A law student

PART II

Write exams like a straight A law student. Get 85-90%.

LAW SCHOOL EXAMS: SECRETS OF STRAIGHT A STUDENT

Legal Writing for Exams Edition

by The Law School Girl

For you, my dear law students.

I've been in your shoes, and I know what it's like to try so hard to become a straight A student all by yourself, not knowing what else to do.

No worries, we are here to divulge all our secrets.

INTRODUCTION

W e've been in your shoes. We know what it's like to give your all and study so hard throughout your law school semester yet have your exam blow all your efforts away. It's not your fault. It's because no one actually teaches you HOW to answer every type of question, word for word. Law professors and the schools keep those secrets hidden. They make success a mystery for you to figure out by yourself as they drown you in useless readings. The sad truth is that employers first look at your grades. No matter how well you understand the law and your legal courses, if you don't have the grades to prove it, your competence will unfortunately not be taken seriously. That's where we come in. We teach you the skills you need to excel in exam writing so you can stand up for yourself and, demonstrate with numbers that you mastered your courses and law degree.

Crafting your law exam answers is a skill. For straight A students, we consider it an art that anyone can learn, with an open mind. A skill can be taught, but first you must learn the art of writing complete and concise answers in your law school exams before you get to doing. For every type of success, comes behind it a strategy. Once you learn the proper strategy, and use your discipline to practice and apply it, we guarantee that your grades will significantly rise to a level you would have never thought you can reach.

We were C and B students before we discovered our secret code which thankfully made us top 2% law students. You can be that too. But you must be very careful about who you learn from. Initially, we were C and B students because the conventional advice out there that WE relied on, and the so called "confidential advice" out there is given by people who did not graduate among the top 2%. We learned that everybody has an opinion and is overly enthusiastic about sharing it, but the real valuable opinions that will *ACTUALLY* make a difference are those of straight A law students, who clearly demonstrated <u>with their results</u> that they know what they are talking about. If you want to learn how to be the best, you must learn from those who cracked the code and actually **became** the BEST. Not average, not mildly successful, not simply "passed" onto to the second or third year but became and graduated top of their class. Here, in our book, you have the chance to pick our brains.

If you have the right study strategy that will catalyze your excellent exam performance as we teach you in our book *"Straight A Student's Guide to Law School"*, the other missing piece that we teach you here, in *"Law School Exams: secrets of straight A students"*, is putting all your course knowledge to writing. There's only a special way to put it in writing that screams to your professor **"I mastered your course!"**, and we will be teaching you that way. If you've been studying wrong this entire semester, this part will be the most difficult for you, which is why we strongly recommend that you save yourself some pain and use our study tips in *"Straight A Student's Guide to Law School"*. On the other hand, if you've been using our study tips, you're now almost set. The only work left is practising (in your practice exams) your writing, like we teach you in this book. Ready? Let's go.

EXAM IS ON THE TABLE. What we recommend doing now is glancing at every question in the exam and at the percentages attributed to each question so you may divide your time accordingly.

FACT-PATTERN QUESTIONS

O n average worth about 40+% of your grade.

Definition: Fact pattern questions give you hypothetical facts about a client that you need to generally advise.

Your job: give them all options with respect to potential legal claims and counter-claims, and hypothetical issues related to those options, no matter how likely or unlikely they are (the options and issues). Then, for each option or issue, you must conclude in one sentence what the degree of likelihood for success is, *IN YOUR OPINION*. Clearly state that it is *YOUR* opinion.

Fact pattern questions are **by far** usually, the **biggest** portion that **counts the most** and is *the* most frequent question in your exams; <u>for the right reasons.</u>

How does a straight A, top 2%, law student answer

fact pattern questions?

(#1) Reading the facts.

When reading the facts, this is **by far the most crucial time** where **your focus must be 100%** lasered and entirely absorbing that information. Understanding the facts wrong or missing a point <u>could potentially ruin your entire performance</u>. We say that from personal experience. **Ever heard of laser focus?** That is what we recommend. Your mind must be completely empty as you read the facts with only the voice of your exam's facts in your mind. That is why we recommended in *"Straight A Student's Guide to Law School"* to **meditate right before the exam**. Meditation puts you in the present moment and empties your mind. It brings your mind out of thinking and focuses it on boring details like your breathing, the tree leaves etc. for a considerable amount of time. Your mind therefore trains on auto-pilot to focus on the details and not be caught up with parasite-like thoughts. The practice of meditation has the powerful effect of making you present in the moment and focused on only what is infront of you, not in your mind, which is very useful when you read fact-pattern questions.

<u>Put yourself in each party's shoes</u> in that factum and make mental notes of each of their issues as if they composed a checklist in your mind. Picture yourself in your parties' shoes and be empathetic towards each one of them as if it were you suffering from those problems. This helps <u>you deeply understand what they might be looking for between the lines</u>, that is how you come up with unique potential solutions, and <u>go the extra mile to provide that extra possible far-fetched</u> yet plausible <u>solution</u> that your classmates didn't even think of. No matter how far-reached your solutions are, professors appreciate uniqueness, persistence in going through *__all__* relevant hypothetical claims and creativity. You'll score extra points for that, I know that from experience.

(#2) Processing.

Your focus is NOT the facts per say, but translating every single possible fact and issue presented in your exam into a recognized legal claim and rule that you studied and have on your course's outline (which you must have been crafting during this entire semester -if the exam is open book). Your professor wants you to use your outline, what you've learned from your syllabus. IT IS NOT ABOUT THE FACTS, but using the law you learned to bring solutions to your clients. Please read "Straight A Student's Guide to Law School" on Amazon.com for more details on **creating the perfect course outline** that will be most effective and helpful to get your straight A on your exams.

So the more often you translate in that way, the more points you score. Thus, ultimately, it is a question of speed in legal translation of as many facts and issues as possible.

(#3) Highlighting.

As you go line by line, understanding the facts and issues in your exam, you will recognize legal claims and issues governed by rules of law that you have previously studied. Use your pencil to lightly circle them or the triggering facts in the exam's text and draw an arrow from that circle all the way to the side of the text where you will write one-word notes of potential applicable LEGAL claims. We suggest using a pencil because sometimes, you will be wrong about the relevancy of your inferences. In that case, you would easily be able to erase mistakes and avoid getting uselessly distracted by them. You may also underline with your pencil a series of legal claims for the same person that are already described in the text as such. Beside the text, we suggest writing numbers like (1),(2),(3),(4) with your pencil to remember all potential claims you must treat in your analysis, in a checklist manner.

Sometimes, you will receive factums already telling you what opposite parties are claiming against each other along with corresponding arguments. <u>Find a way to visually separate these two op-posite claims with your highlighter,</u> by using a different color for each party. I, for example, use two different highlighting colors to separate what each party is arguing against the other so I can remember to treat both sides without confusing them. I barely and lightly highlight a sentence or two in the biggest claims just to draw my attention back to those while I'm writing. **Remember not to over-highlight for example an entire paragraph**. This can blur your vision and make you miss other very important, yet non highlighted items, in the text. Remember also to continue creating a code: the biggest parts and arguments should be under-scored in a more attention-grabbing manner than sub-points or sub-issues. For example, sometimes I highlight with the full brush for an extremely important point, then I use just the tip of the highlighter to emphasize a sub-point that is relatively less important compared to the first point yet still crucial to mention overall. This way you would be already creating a mental flow-chart for your answers.

At other times, **you will receive factums not telling you any-thing about what each party is claiming against the other.** Keep highlighting and noting the legal claims that you notice in the text, just from reading the facts.

That is what I received in Contracts and earned an A for. You will be asked to imagine **all** of the possible relevant claims yourself. *That is fine, relax.* That is where your empathy and imagination come in to describe what each party can potentially claim given the listed facts that are pro-one party or the other. In this case, I like to <u>divide solutions into scenarios</u>. I use as the following title for the first part of my answer "Scenario I" and draft the big poten-tial claims my client can make against the other party as well as the ones the opposing party can raise against ours, **in full detail**. If there is another scenario of claims, then I use as a title for the sec-ond part: "Scenario II" and, I draft the second big potential claims under that scenario and still treat that in full detail with the same blueprint as the first scenario. Usually, in Contracts, Scenario I may be about a certain way that a party interprets a contract and the opposite ways that the opposing party may counter-claim. Scenario II, in this case, would be a whole other way that that first party may interpret the contract and the relevant counter-claims and opposing impressions that the opposing party may respectively make and be under. Oh yes, there will be several for each party; it will be long, but hang in there and keep writing. **Treat ALL OF THEM. DO NOT MAKE THE MISTAKE OF ONLY WRITING THE MOST LIKELY SCENARIOS. THAT IS NOT WHAT YOUR PROFESSOR WANTS.**

Imagine that you missed Scenario II because you forgot to even think about it as you were under the impression that you wrote a lot for Scenario I, you would have missed *half* of your points. That is why we urge you, in our first part of the *Straight A Law Student* series, *"Straight A Student's Guide to Law School"*, to think of ALL the possible hypothetical situations arising from a certain set of facts as you study cases throughout the entire semester. We teach you to prepare for this from the beginning of the semester. If you listened to our advice, it should be quick for you to imagine Scenarios II in the exam, as well as to make sure you note down on your exam sheet to treat it later.

(#4) READ VERY CAREFULLY THE QUESTION AT THE BOTTOM.

It determines how you answer and the scope or bias of your answer. Pay very close attention to what the professor is asking of you. The reason for that is self-evident, if you ask us.

(#5) WRITING YOUR ANSWERS.

Unless your professor specifically requests a specific method of legal analysis and writing, **you can never go wrong with the IRAC method**. It organizes your legal writing and analysis, making it much easier for you to get an A. It also helps you analyze and write quicker, since all of your answers will always be organized under the same efficient blueprint: The IRAC.

Here's what **IRAC** stands for:

I= Issue

R= Rule

A= Applicability

C= Conclusion

Those 4 elements represent how you must organize your answer to your fact-pattern exam question. Every legal issue and sub-issue that your fact-pattern raises must be treated according to the IRAC rule. Hence you will be repeating those 4 elements numerous times (to say the least…) in your exam, because fact-patterns are loaded with issues that need to be dealt with according to IRAC, one by one.

They key to success here, usually isn't applying the IRAC rule itself, but **remembering to deal with ALL issues in the text including minor ones.** It is very easy to completely forget about the rest of the issues while you use IRAC for one. Nevertheless, your professor expects you to deal with *all* issues to get an A. They write your fact-pattern questions with already an idea in mind of every legal issue to be addressed. So how do you remember to treat all issues? First, think of yourself as a surgeon dissecting every piece of that text and filtering every possible legal issue you can find that matches a rule or ratio in a case that you studied throughout your semester. Remember our advice above to note with your pencil potential claims? That's where *that* becomes useful. But sometimes you need more, and that's where your geniusely crafted course outline and study method come in. Remember in *"Straight A Student Guide to Law School"*, where we advise you to summarise every case in one sentence and write the main themes of your course on your outline throughout your semester? Thanks to drafting such a small outline yet with so much information on one page, you can browse through quickly the entire outline and glance at all rules, during your exam, to make sure that you haven't missed any potential argument or counter-argument that you may add in your answer. **I did that in Contracts, when I wanted to go that extra mile and received an A.**

APPLYING THE **IRAC** RULE:

From our experience, **I** and **A** are *the* most important parts of IRAC.

To put **IRAC** to practice, here's an example of how you start writing your very first sentence in your exam:

*TIP: DO NOT REWRITE FACTS, DIRECTLY START WITH "**I**" (Issue).*

I: *"The issue is whether Mary has a claim for …"*.

Here, you repeat what is asked of you if you are asked whether your client has a particular claim. If you're not specifically asked about the viability of a specific claim, you still need to figure out whether there is some viable claim, <u>so you start with your first hypothetical potential claim</u>.

R: *"The rule* (state the section, case name or whichever) *states that a person asking for* (insert legal right) *must satisfy the following four elements:* (insert criteria, with each criterion followed by the case name that imposed or described the criterion)".

A: *"In our case,* (state the relevant facts that make it likely or not that your rule applies or not), *which means that/therefore it is likely or not very likely* that (state whether the rule in question applies to the facts you just mentioned/ whether the legal test or each legal criterion of the test in met for each point).

> TIP: Mention the NAMES of the clients or parties
> the rule applies or doesn't to, and get the names
> right, don't confuse them. You should demonstrate
> attention to details and focus to your professor.

C: Conclude in one sentence overall whether the claim is viable or not **in your opinion** (easiest and quickest part not to waste time on). There is no wrong or right opinion here, you only need to make sure your opinion matches logically what you have said in parts I, R and A of the IRAC blueprint.

Here is an example of an answer that requires addressing multiple sub-issues and that includes rules with many requirements for a test:

I: *"The issue is whether Mary has a claim for ..."*.

Here, again, you rephrase what is asked of you if you are asked whether your client has a claim. If you're not specifically asked about the viability of a specific claim, you still need to figure out whether there is some viable claim, so you start with your first hypothetical potential claim.

Next:

"In order to determine whether she/he does, the first issue is whether...".

Here, you go into your first sub-issue.

R: *"The rule* (reference the section number, case name or whichever) *states that a person asking for* (insert legal right) *must satisfy the following four elements: 1.* (State the name of the element briefly with the case name that imposed it between brackets, if different than the rule mentionned above), *2.* (idem), *3.* (idem), and *4.* (idem).".

Follow by treating element 1: "(Insert case name) *provides that the plaintiff must have* (insert rule) *to meet the element 1 criterion*".

Explain what a case provides about how to determine whether it is met or not. Then apply part A of IRAC.

Repeat the same process with elements 2, 3, and 4... etc. When you're done with all elements, conclude whether the main test is overall met (part C of IRAC).

A: *"In our case, Mary did this -or that-* (state the relevant facts that make it likely or not that your rule applies or not), *which means that/therefore it is likely or not very likely for* (state the rule yet apply it to the facts that you just mentioned).

> TIP: Mention the NAMES of the clients or parties the rule applies or doesn't to, and <u>get the names right, don't confuse them.</u> You should demonstrate attention to detail and focus to your professor.

C: (easiest and quickest part not to waste time on).

ANOTHER EFFECTIVE TIP:

Professor Eric E. Johnson, who graduated with a JD from Harvard Law School, explained *so* effectively the IRAC method in a way that it flipped a switch in my head and, helped me ace every law exam I took after applying his advice. Shoutout to Professor Johnson! He says that the golden key to success that helps us ace law school exams is mainly <u>applying the law to facts</u>, which I completely agree with as I received straight As by focusing on this point of view. This is *the* only way to show that you understand the law. He explains that <u>in order to create perfect legal analysis,</u>

you necessarily must mix the law and the facts together in a way that produces some result.

Consider the following color **metaphor:**

red + blue = purple

If law is blue and facts are red, then you want to make purple. Remember: **making purple is golden.**

Professor Johnson, thank you so much for helping us get straight As in Law School.

Now, below, are examples of how you apply Professor Johnson's genius golden purple rule to the IRAC method, because this is what you need to accomplish in order to succeed.

CRIMINAL LAW:

(Excerpt of your hypothetical exam's facts in RED: <Abby shouted "That saw blade is going to hit you!" to Danny.>)

Issue (PURPLE): The issue is whether <Mary> RED has a claim for <assault> BLUE against <Danny> RED.

Rule (BLUE): The rule (reference the number or name of the relevant rule that you should find on your outline) states that there must be an immediate apprehension of harmful touching (or a more general element that you then specify through examples) for a valid assault claim.

Application (PURPLE): In our case, <Danny shouted to Abby warning her about a saw blade about to hit her> RED, which could highly likely create for <Abby> RED an <immediate apprehension of harmful touching> BLUE.

Conclusion (PURPLE): Therefore, Abby likely has a solid claim for assault against Danny.

TORTS:

(Excerpt of your hypothetical exam's facts in RED: <The school wants to sue Peter for negligence. (…) Although Peter had been intoxicated in the gymnasium, the latter was already burning and the roof fell apart>)

Issue (PURPLE): *The issue is whether* <*the school*> RED *can prove* <*actual causation under the but-for test*> BLUE.

Rule (BLUE): *The case* (state the name) *provides that* (define the but-for test and the necessity of causation).

Application (PURPLE): *In our case,* <*The gymnasium would have burned anyway, even if Peter was not intoxicated*> RED, *which means that* <*the gymnasium would not have burned but-for the intoxication of Peter*> PURPLE.

Conclusion (PURPLE): *It is therefore unlikely that the element of causation will be satisfied in our case*.

Remember that your goal in answering these questions, is citing and referencing as many rules and cases as possible to apply to your exam's facts. The bulk of your exam points is attributed to your skill in applying the law you studied in your courses to facts. You should mostly pay attention to the "**A**" part of the **IRAC** rule because professors are mostly interested in your opinion of whether the law is likely to help your client or not. In other words, professors want to ultimately know whether you think you have a legal claim or not, and **WHY**. <u>WHY</u>, is actually more important than the conclusion of having a valid claim or not, and that is where you should relax; there is no right or wrong answer when it comes to having a legal claim or not, which is the *best* positive news you can get. If it's all about why there might or might not be a legal claim, then you can use your entire creativity to write how facts could be interpreted in one or other ways which might both make your claim plausible and non plausible at the same time! Fun, isn't it? Don't worry when you reach such opposing hypothetical demonstrations on your paper, your professor actually wants to see that you caught the various conflicting potential interpretations. That is where you score the most points. Sometimes professors give you vague facts *on purpose*: to see if you will catch the wide variety of options in legal analysis. Professors test here how far and creative a law student's thinking goes to think of all potential legal issues.

There is a very simple way to conclude such situations after writing your many possibilities (e.g. Going back to the Torts example above *"On the other hand, it is possible that the facts could be interpreted in a way as such that although the wildfire was not Peter's fault, it is only his intoxication that may have aggravated -a particular- situation making* -another rule on your outline thus syllabus-*applicable).* To conclude, simply state your opinion about which theory is more likely to be admitted by judges and give at least one logical reason for it. Remember, no right or wrong answer, professors will look at the reasons for which you made your conclusions, not the substance of the conclusion itself.

Here's an example of a conclusion: *"That being said, I think that the first interpretation is more likely to succeed because <it is more common knowledge that (...)> or <it is more reasonable for (facts to have gone one way not the other...)> or <judges have previously ruled X on similar cases or situations in (insert case name)> etc.".*

Where do you draw the line on expanding on hypothetical situations? The rule of thumb in fact-pattern questions is to only EXPAND on hypothetical situations when it implies that different rules from your your outline (syllabus) will apply causing a different possible result or conclusion. Another rule of thumb is that when facts are missing to decide one way or the other, state that they are missing. State _what_ exactly is missing, but do not invent facts to make your interpretation go a certain direction.

You may write analyses such as "*if facts were (this way) then the rule would apply (that way), and Mary would end up with no claim. However, if facts were (that way) then the rule would be in Mary's favor*". However, I do not recommend expanding further than this for such cases because not all professors add points for such sentences, but some do.

So the key premise, that you must absolutely bring with you to your exam while answering fact-pattern questions, is that the facts ARE NOT there to trick you and mislead you. Your focus is not THE FACTS, in and of themselves. The focus is on taking those facts and seeing how they may translate into laws applying. Do these facts help form a legal claim? The legal claim, in order for it to succeed, needs certain criteria to be met. Are the criteria met, given our facts?

Don't be afraid of writing that you need more facts to prove a specific criterion. Your professors actually expect this from you. When you don't do this, you will lose points because professors will note that you didn't notice the *issue* they wanted you to notice. Professors will give you vague facts ON PURPOSE because they want to see if you will pretend that the facts are enough for you to draw a conclusion or whether, in real life, you would need to know more details before concluding about the applicability of a legal criterion. I cannot stress this enough.

Define. Define.

Definitions here are **important.** On a scale from 1 to 10, they are level 8 important. When do you define? Here's an example:

"*The rule "X" states that the accused must have the requisite mens rea and actus reus before being charged. Mens rea is* (definition, in one sentence). *Actus reus is* (definition, in one sentence)."

From this example, you can see that you must define legal terms used in rules that you reference for the first time on your paper (or in your answer, if you're typing on a computer). **Straight A stu-**

dents define the terms they use, B students forget to do that.

ESSAY QUESTIONS

Essay questions, from my experience, are the second most important and frequent questions that appear on law school exams. On average worth about 15-30% of your grade.

Definition: essay questions generally ask your opinion about the fairness and logic of a rule, doctrine or a case. The question will not necessarily be phrased in that specific and direct way, it will most likely ask you to critically analyze a certain rule or doctrine. Sometimes, the question will be more direct in asking you to compare to different doctrines or rules. Overall, your opinion is asked.

<u>Your job:</u>

1. Is to have a strong opinion.

2. IS to criticize by using arguments based on sections of rules, case ratios or arguments, as well as doctrines. Here, again, there is no such thing as a right or wrong answer. You just need to have a strong opinion about whether a doctrine or rule is useful in achieving X goal or not.

How do you get a strong opinion? Obviously, you don't build it during the exam itself.

If you have been following our advice from *"Straight A Student's Guide to Law School"*, YOU HAVE NOTHING TO FEAR because you've been practising your answer to this question all semester. We prepared you for this. YOU SHOULD HAPPILY AWAIT THIS QUESTION. That's where you enjoy the fruits of your regular effort in thinking independently about rules and cases throughout the semester. This is what we taught you to prepare for in detail in *"Straight A Student's Guide to Law School"*.

When critically thinking about a rule or doctrine, we recommend that you focus on two things:

1. The original intent behind creating the law or doctrine, and

2. Its consequences.

We suggest and recommend focusing on the following questions to build your constructive criticism:

- How fair is this rule to its subordinates? If the rule is based on equity, a focus on fairness is highly warranted.
- What problems is the rule or doctrine causing?
- How useful is the rule?
- What is the rule's goal?
- Why was the doctrine created in the first place? To what aim? Is it achieving it?
- Has the doctrine been modified over-time? List how and why each modification took place, as well as how it solved the issues it was aiming to remedy and not.
- How efficient is the rule ?
- How accurate is the doctrine?
- Is the doctrine still relevant?
- What changes are needed today for the rule or doctrine to be more useful, efficient, fair or up to date? Be creative here.

- How does it affect society in general?
- What would you do differently? Be honest and direct, don't be shy to say your true opinion. That is personally my favorite part about this question, as I can apply my imagination and creativity.
- Is the scope of the rule or doctrine sufficient?
- Is the rule overbroad? Why?
- Is a part of society excluded and left in an unknown situation due to the rule?
- Where do you see the doctrine or rule going in the near future? That is a different question than what you would like to see happening. It is rather a question about the consequences that may get aggravated or otherwise in the future.

Hopefully those key few pointers help you steer your essay towards a certain direction. After all, professors just want a certain clear direction (aka your opinion).

Even though your opinion is required, you must give examples from your legislation, cases and name of doctrines that you used. So visually speaking, I would say about every two sentences needs to have a legal reference. Obviously, this is a rough approximation and it surely varies, however this is only to illustrate to you that you simply cannot neglect the legal referencing part of your answer to the extent of only citing two examples in your entire essay. Aim for at least 5 legal references per essay question, if you can.

When you feel a little bit lost, browse through your course outline, and glance at relevant rules. This may help you come up with new arguments and references if your mind goes blank.

In *"Straight A Student's Guide to Law School"*, we recommended a specific way to highlight your textbook materials. If your essay question is about the evolution of a doctrine (-Remember, even though it is about the evolution which is rather factual, your critical opinion about it and its consequences is requested), reach out to your textbook which should be already highlighted according to *"Straight A Student's Guide to Law School"*, and go to the relevant pages and headlines to make sure you've mentioned all of the important reasons for which the doctrine was created. Our mind can only remember so many things, so cross-checking with your textbook is a good idea.

DO NOT freak out if your essay question is about a doctrine you did not bother studying throughout your semester; this not an issue if your exam is open book. In *"Straight A Student's Guide to Law School"*, we taught you to protect yourself from such situations. Open your textbook, search for the doctrine, and focus on the sentences mentioning WHY the doctrine was established in the first place. Then, using your outline, think of the consequences as mentioned in the list of questions above.

Throughout the semester, we also strongly recommend asking questions to your professor about their essay question. Ask them how they expect you to answer it, whether there will be an essay question in the exam or not.

In terms of following a formal structure for your answer to your essay question, we do not find this as important as the content itself. The essay question is not aiming for a formal research paper, it is simply here to confirm that you have critically thought about your course's rules, and that you have a strong opinion about the consequences or changes that must be made. Focus on the content of your essay and the flow of your logical arguments. The overall structure of your answer should look like: **definitions** (please define every rule or doctrine you mention) – **critique about origin/consequence – what you would do differently**.

Define. Define. Define.

Definitions here are very important, to say the least. On a scale from 1 to 10, we would say 9.5. Make sure to define every doctrine that you are referencing for the first time, and explain its scope of application. Professors enjoy it when your paper can be understood by a 5 year old. Try your best to consider that your professor is not a legal expert. Define, define, define.

CASE COMMENTARY QUESTIONS

May vary between being worth 10-30% of your exam, or otherwise being a home exam in the form of a research paper.

Definition: case commentary questions ask you to analyze a case. More directly, they may ask you what you would have decided in a case if you were the judge or justice.

<u>Your job:</u> is to get creative by modifying the ratio to your heart's desire and writing your own arguments about it.

Obviously, you will not exclusively write your own arguments from scratch. You may alter between rephrasing the arguments in the case that you agree on, adding an extra idea that you see fit, and adding an entire argument that you thought of from scratch.

Luckily, you don't need to define things here, unless it is relevant to your new arguments (e.g. if a definition should logically include a group of people in your opinion, defining the term in question is important to make your argument so you can prove that logically, the group you're considering should be included). The focus of the answer to this question should be on your opinion and arguments.

The *good news* about this question is that the initial instinctive reaction you get from reading the ratio could serve as the basis for your answer. When I was writing my Contracts exam, such a question came up. I completely modified the ratio of the case. The ratio defined a term in what I thought was very a limited way. It was trying to create change but it practically didn't because it did not completely innovate and recategorize the groups. It excluded a group of people who deserved to be protected by the rule. So my initial out-of-the-box (mental and personal) opinion of how the definition should also include another group of people traditionally defined as "different" for logical and fairness purposes (which was the initial motive for the ratio in the first place) was my answer to this question. I got an A. Now I did not just write what I thought should be done, I wrote that and also my logical arguments proving that there is no evidence suggesting that my proposal should not logically be implemented. In other words, I demonstrated with legal arguments that logic dictates that my idea should not be considered.

Going with the dissent or majority.

For case commentary questions we do not recommend agreeing with the majority or the dissent and ending it there. Most of your classmates will do that. Thus, your paper is not likely to stand out. If you're desperate, you may go ahead and do that; but at least add new arguments to either the dissent or majority. The ideal would be adding three new arguments. The more sub-arguments (obviously legal with legal references), the better. But make sure to focus on three main arguments.

Innovate.

Instead, we recommend this: don't be afraid to write something you think is far-reached and completely different. If your professor asks you such a question in your exam, they are testing your creative skills in crafting a law, and your logical skills in legally arguing for it. Once again, your outline (the one we've been teaching you to prepare in "Straight A Student's Guide to Law School") will help you back your opinion and arguments with legal rules. You must cite at least some legal reference, if you can, here. The more legal references you make here, the better, and the higher your score. Because although judges do decide based on emotion and moral considerations to some extent, they use legal references as excuses. That is what your professor is teaching you to do through this question: to have an opinion but use the law to advocate for it. This is not a question where you put forward traditional thinking, the more odd and different your proposal is, yet LOGICAL, the more your answer will stand out to your professor. You can't answer the same way most of your classmates answer (which is probably the obvious way). You must be courageous in advancing something new, and different. Usually, those are the ideas that you think people would think are ridiculous, yet they won't be able to find a flaw in your logic for. Those are usually the best answers.

If you have not read yet our book *"Straight A Student's Guide to Law School"*, now is the time to do it. You cannot get an A in your exam exclusively with writing skills if you have not even organized the examinable content of your course in the most efficient way possible to use quickly during your exam, as we explore in *"Straight A Student's Guide to Law School"*.

If you have any questions, feel free to write us, WE WILL REPLY.

You can email us at: info.lawschoolgirl@gmail.com

If you've found this book useful, please consider writing a review on Amazon.com

Thank you for helping us.

We would like to spread the message that professors and law schools must stop being so mysterious when it comes to success.

For daily motivational quotes and out-of-the-box food for thought in law school,

check out our instagram page: @thelawschoolgirl

Made in the USA
Middletown, DE
03 January 2020

82527279R00020